Celebrating Ramadan

رمضان المعظم
١٤٢١

by Diane Hoyt-Goldsmith

photographs by Lawrence Migdale

Holiday House / New York

Library of Congress Cataloging-in-Publication Data
Hoyt-Goldsmith, Diane.
    Celebrating Ramadan / by Diane Hoyt-Goldsmith, photographs by Lawrence Migdale.
       p. cm.
    ISBN 0-8234-1581-3 (hardcover)   ISBN 0-8234-1762-X (paperback)
      1. Ramadan—Juvenile literature. 2. Islam—Rituals—Juvenile Literature. [1. Ramadan.
2. Fasts and feasts—Islam.] I. Migdale, Lawrence, ill. II. Title.

BP186.4 .H69 2001
297. '62—dc21   2001016643

This book is dedicated to
Ibraheem's grandparents:
Saffet and Sarah Catovic and
Abdel-Rehim and Nagda Riad.
Their faith and tireless commitment to
their families and community
make them ideal role models
for their children and grandchildren,
and anyone fortunate enough
to know them.

Acknowledgments
We would like to thank many people for making it possible to create this book. First of all, we would like to thank the Catovic Family, Saffet Abid, Abir, Ibraheem, Ismael, and Mariam. In the days since this book was begun, there is a new member of the family: Sarah Nagda, born on October 26, 2000. Thanks also to Ibraheem's grandparents, Saffet and Sarah Catovic and Abdel-Rehim and Nagda Riad. We enjoyed sharing the Eid breakfast at the home of Saffiya and Behram Turan with their children Muhammed Emin, Mustafa, Osman, Omer, and Meryem. The rest of the family always made us feel welcome and were very helpful. We are grateful to Suada and Moutaz Charaf and their children, Aziza, Ali, Ammar, and Hasan; to Surayya Catovic and Ahmad Haj-Ibrahim and their children, Salma, Tameem, and Salwa; to Amira Riad and Magdy Hagag and their children, Abdurrahman and Halima; to Sami Catovic; to Kassem and Nany Riad and their children, Tammer, Yasser, and Rania.

    We greatly appreciate the cooperation of the Board of Trustees and members of The Islamic Society of Central Jersey, and the teachers, staff, and students of the Noor-Ul-Iman School. We would like to give a special thank-you to Imam Hamad Chebli, the Religious Leader of The Islamic Society of Central Jersey, for the cooperation and welcome that we received.

    Finally, we wish to thank Shabbir Mansuri of the Council on Islamic Education, and Susan Douglass, the reviewer, for their guidance in the development of this book and for the review of the manuscript to ensure that the text is accurate and reflects the values of the Muslim community.

Mohamed Zakariya, calligrapher
Mohamed Zakariya is an Islamic calligrapher, artist, master woodworker, and engraver. Born in Ventura, California, in 1942, he began his study of Islamic calligraphy with A.S. Ali Nour in Tangier and London in 1964. After continuing his studies at the British Museum, he was invited to Istanbul to study with two celebrated Turkish calligraphers, Hasan Celebi anf Ali Alparslan. In recognition of his accomplishments and ability, Mohamed Zakariya is the first American to earn the prized *icazet* (diploma) from Mr. Celebi in 1988 and Mr. Alparslan in 1997. Mr. Zakariya's calligraphy has been exhibited widely both in this country and abroad. He has exhibited his calligraphy and given demonstrations in conjunction with "Al-Andalus: The Art of Islamic Spain" at the Metropolitan Museum of Art in New York City. One of this works is now in the collection of the Calligraphy Museum of Türkpetrol Vakfi in Istanbul, one of the finest private museums of Islamic calligraphic art in the world. Mr. Zakariya also designs and contructs functioning examples of horological and scientifc instruments, including astrolabes. The calligraphy created for the title page of this book is written in Arabic. The translation reads: "Ramadan, the Revered and Magnificent."

Ibraheem (ib-rah-HEEM) is in the fourth grade and lives near Princeton, New Jersey. Like five million other Americans, Ibraheem is a Muslim. He and his family follow the way of life and religion of Islam (is-LAHM). Each year they fast for the month of Ramadan (rah-mah-DAHN), one of Islam's most important celebrations. For more than 1400 years, people all over the world who follow Islam have been celebrating Ramadan. With the start of Ramadan, Muslims begin a month-long period of fasting. They do not drink or eat anything during the daylight hours. Muslims do this to show their faith in God, called Allah (ah-LAH) in the Arabic language, and to show obedience to God's commands. By fasting, they also share the experience of those people who are poor. Ramadan is a time to make amends. It is a time when Muslims end disputes and show kindness to everyone.

The Five Pillars of Islam

Shahada

(shah-HAH-dah)
Declaration of Belief
A Muslim declares that there is but one God,
Allah, and Muhammad is His Prophet.

Salat

(sah-LAHT)
Prayer
Five times each day,
Muslims pray to Allah.

Sawm

(SAHWM)
Fasting
For one month called Ramadan,
all adult Muslims fast,
which means they do not eat or drink
anything during the daylight hours,
to show their obedience to Allah.

Zakat

(zah-KAHT)
Poor's Due
All Muslims give money or goods,
to purify their wealth
and help others.

Hajj

(HAHJ)
Pilgrimage
All Muslims who are able,
travel to Makkah, Islam's holiest site,
at least once in their lives.

The Religion of Islam

Three religions devoted to one all-powerful God arose in the desert lands of the Middle East. These are Judaism, Christianity, and Islam. Muslims believe that the prophets of Judaism and Christianity, including Abraham, Moses, David, and Jesus, are great prophets. (They are called Ibraheem, Musa, Dawood, and Isa in Arabic.) Their stories are included in Islam's holy book, the Qur'an (kur-AHN). For Muslims, the last and most important prophet was Muhammad (mu-HAHM-mad), who was a descendent of Abraham.

The new religion of Islam brought great social change to the world that existed in the seventh century. During Muhammad's time, people living in the desert lands of the Middle East faced many hardships. Food and water were scarce, and feuds between tribes were common. In those days, people worshiped many different gods.

Islam brought peace and harmony to the people of the Arabian peninsula. The word Islam is an Arabic word that means "peace" and "submission to God." Muslims believe in living according to God's commands. At the same time, they are tolerant of other people and their beliefs. As they came to follow Islam, the many warring tribes in Arabia were united under one religion and one God for the first time. Finally people could live in peace and harmony.

For Muslims, Islam is a way of life as well as a religion. The most important ways to worship God and follow His commandments are found in the "Five Pillars of Islam." These are the basic requirements each Muslim must follow. They ensure that Islam is a part of every believer's daily routine.

RUSSIA

KAZAKHSTAN MONGOLIA

AZERBAIJAN
GEORGIA
ARMENIA

BOSNIA

UZBEKISTAN
KYRGYZSTAN

TURKMENISTAN

TAJIKISTAN CHINA

TURKEY

TUNISIA
CYPRUS SYRIA
IRAQ IRAN
AFGHANISTAN

MOROCCO

ESTERN
AHARA ALGERIA LIBYA
EGYPT
KUWAIT
JORDAN
PAKISTAN BANGLADESH

ITANIA INDIA

SAUDI ARABIA
•Makkah (Mecca) UNITED
ARAB
EMIRATES

MALI
NIGER CHAD
SUDAN YEMEN OMAN

ETHIOPIA

SOMALIA

INDONESIA

(Above) Many of the world's more than one billion Muslims live in countries where Islam is the dominant religion, shown in green on the map. These are the lands to which Islam spread in centuries past and where diverse Muslim cultures have developed.

(Left) Ibraheem's mother was born in Egypt. She came to the United States with her family when she was eight years old. Ibraheem's father was born in the United States. His father immigrated to the United States from Bosnia, a country in Eastern Europe. Ibraheem's grandmother was born in the United States and converted to Islam.

5

The Five Daily Prayers

Fajr is performed from dawn until just before sunrise.

Zuhr is performed after midday until midafternoon.

Asr is performed from midafternoon until late afternoon.

Maghrib is performed after sunset.

Isha is a night prayer, performed in the first third of the night after twilight.

Ibraheem and his family, like Muslims all over the world, pray to Allah five times every day. Although Muslims pray wherever they find themselves, they like to pray together as a community whenever possible. People leave their homes and offices and come to a place called a masjid (MAHS-jid) or mosque to pray. Located a few miles away from Ibraheem's home, the masjid has a tower called a minaret (MIN-ah-rhet). Traditionally, a minaret is the place where a person climbs to call other believers to prayer. The round dome on the roof, called Quba (CU-bah) in Arabic, is located above the large room, empty of all furniture, where Muslims can pray together.

The masjid is more than a place of worship. People also come here for meetings, to take classes, and to enjoy meals together during times of celebration.

Once a week on Friday at midday, Muslims in the whole community gather in the masjid to pray together. People enter after first removing their shoes. Before coming to pray, each person performs wudu (woo-DOO), a ritual of washing hands, face, and feet. In doing this, they follow the practice of Prophet Muhammad and the teachings of the Qur'an. They form long straight rows to pray, shoulder-to-shoulder with one another. The men and boys pray in the front of the room, facing in the direction of Makkah (MAK-kah), a city in Saudi Arabia. Women and girls pray in a separate area, following a centuries old tradition of separating the sexes. Although they pray separately, women and men are equal in Islam. Muslims believe that everyone, rich or poor, young and old, is equal before Allah.

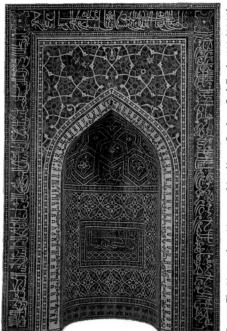

(Above) The mihrab (MIH-rahb) is a niche built into the wall of the masjid. Often it is decorated with fine mosaics or beautifully painted tiles. The mihrab is placed so that when Muslims face toward it during prayer, they will be facing toward Makkah.

(Left) Ibraheem sits next to his grandfather for the evening prayer inside the masjid.

The Revelations of Muhammad

Long ago in the desert land of Arabia, there lived a man named Muhammad. Although he started life as an orphan, he was destined to change the world. After Muhammad's parents died, his grandfather, an important Makkan leader, took him into his home and raised him as if he were a son. After he died, Muhammad's uncle took him in.

Like many of the prophets, Muhammad worked as a shepherd when he was a child. After he grew older, he traveled with the caravans to Palestine and Syria to trade. Later, he worked for a businesswoman who owned caravans. Muhammad married her, and they had six children together.

In Muhammad's time, most people in the city of Makkah worshiped many different gods. Muhammad, however, believed in only one God, called Allah.

Throughout his life, Muhammad was quiet and thoughtful. He was always polite and truthful, which earned him the name al-Amin, which means "the trustworthy."

Muhammad always worked hard to support his family. When his work was finished, however, he spent many hours in a cave near his home meditating on Allah and the ways of the world. One day, while he was in the cave, he heard someone call his name.

Muhammad was frightened. He did not realize that the voice came from the angel Jibril (Jib-REEL), called Gabriel in the Bible. In the days and weeks that followed this first encounter, the angel revealed to Muhammad the first verses of what would become the Qur'an. Over the next twenty-three years, Allah sent Jibril to Muhammad to reveal the entire contents of the sacred book of Islam.

After only three years, Allah told Muhammad that he was also to be a Rasul (rah-SOOL) or Messenger. Muhammad began to preach Allah's truth to all who would listen.

As the number of Muslim believers grew, the rich and powerful people in Makkah began to fear these religious teachings. They began to persecute, or cause suffering, to Muhammad and those who followed his teaching.

Islam soon spread to a city some distance away. Muslims in that place offered to welcome the Makkah Muslims to live in their city. The city soon had a new name:

Madinat un-Nabi (mah-DEE-nat un-NAH-bee), which means City of the Prophet. Here, the number of Muslim believers continued to grow.

In 628 CE, the Prophet Muhammad led a large group of his followers to Makkah for the annual pilgrimage or hajj. They were refused entrance to the city until Muhammad negotiated a truce that included allowing his followers to come to Makkah once each year for the hajj.

After a time, the people of Makkah broke the agreement. Then Muhammad led his people against the Makkans, defeating them in battle. Muhammad took his followers to the Kaaba (KAH-bah), a place of worship built by Ibraheem and his first son, Ismael, hundreds of years earlier. It had since become a storehouse for pagan idols and statues. Together, Muhammad and his followers removed the idols from the Kaaba. He rededicated the Kaaba to the worship of one God, Allah. Since those days, most of the people in Makkah have become Muslims and the new religion called Islam has spread throughout the world.

The Islamic Calendar

Ramadan is the name of the ninth month in the Islamic calendar. The Islamic calendar is lunar, based on the phases of the moon. Each of the twelve months begins with the appearance of a new moon and consists of 29 or 30 days to make a total of 354 days in a year.

Ramadan is an important month in the Islamic calendar because it marks the time when the Prophet Muhammad began to receive the revelations of the Qur'an. The first day of the next month, Shawwaal, brings the celebration of the Eid al-Fitr or "Feast of Breaking the Fast." The tenth day of Zul-hijja brings the celebration of the Eid al-Adha or "Feast of the Sacrifice." This commemorates Ibraheem's willingness to sacrifice Ismael for the sake of his faith in Allah. These two are the most important religious holidays for Muslims.

Months in the Islamic Calendar

1. Muharram	7. Rajab
2. Safar	8. Sha-aban
3. Rabi I	9. Ramadan
4. Rabi II	10. Shawwaal
5. Jumada I	11. Zul-qi'adah
6. Jumada II	12. Zul-hijja

The Qur'an

Even though Ibraheem and his family are Americans and speak English at home, they have learned to speak and read Arabic in order to read the Qur'an. They also use Arabic when they pray.

The Qur'an, one of the world's most beautiful and poetic books, contains the revelations of Allah to Prophet Muhammad. During Muhammad's lifetime, all the verses were learned and recited aloud from memory. They were also written down in Arabic. After Muhammad's death, the written copies were collected, checked, and corrected against the recitations.

In Arabic, there are
fifty names for the Qur'an
and ninety-nine names for Allah.

Muslim families rely upon special lunar calendars to set the times for prayer. Ibraheem's brother, Ismael, and his mother check the calendar. As the seasons change throughout the year, the daylight and evening hours change, so the times for prayer change as well.

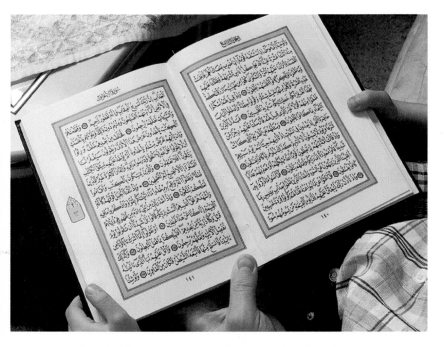

Like children in many other Muslim families, Ibraheem will try to read the entire Qur'an from beginning to end during Ramadan.

Ibraheem's mother, like other Muslim women, covers her head and wears modest , body-concealing clothing. A person's style of dress, however, is determined by the traditions of the country they are from. For example, Egyptian Muslim women wear a head scarf like Ibraheem's mother. Muslim women from other African countries, however, might cover their heads with a turban instead.

Each copy of the Qur'an is exactly the same, word for word. This means that there is only one version of this holy book, the same for all time, in use by those who follow Islam.

Many Muslims know all or a portion of the Qur'an by heart. Verses from the Qur'an are recited during each prayer.

Praying to Allah

No matter where they are, Muslims the world over always pray in the same way. They begin with the "call to prayer." Ibraheem faces toward Makkah in Saudi Arabia. He puts both hands to his ears and calls out these words in Arabic.

The Call to Prayer

Allahu Akbar.
(ah-LAH-hoo AK-bahr)
(Allah is most great.)
Allahu Akbar.
Allahu Akbar.
Allahu Akbar.

I testify there is no god
except Allah.
I testify there is no god
except Allah.
I testify that Muhammad
is the messenger of Allah.
I testify that Muhammad
is the messenger of Allah.
Come to prayer. Come to prayer.
Come to success
(in this life and the Hereafter)!
Come to success!
Allah is most great.
Allah is most great.
There is no god except Allah.

1

1. Ibraheem recites the Al-Fatihah, the first chapter of the Qur'an, which he knows by heart.

2

2. Next he bows, saying:
   Allahu Akbar.
Three times he says:
   Glory to my Lord, the Great.
This position is called Ruku (roo-KOO).

3

3. Then Ibraheem stands up, saying:
   Allah hears those who praise him.
   Our Lord praise to you.
This standing is called Qi'yam (kee-YAM).

4

4. Next Ibraheem kneels with his feet, hands, and forehead touching the ground. He says:
   Allahu Akbar.
Then he says:
   Glory to my Lord, the Highest.
He repeats this three times. This position is called Sujud (soo-JOOD).

5

5. Ibraheem says:
   Allahu Akbar.
He gets up from the floor and sits with his knees bent and palms placed on them.
After a moment's rest, he says:
   Allahu Akbar,
and begins the Sujud again.

The completion of steps 1-5 makes up one ra'kah (RAH-kah) or one unit of salah (sah-LAH) or prayer. For the different prayers during the day, a different number of ra'kat are required.

A large part of each prayer offered to Allah is meant for His praise and glorification, but the prayer also includes asking for guidance and for blessings. After the completion of the required number of ra'kat, Muslims may also say a special, personal prayer called a dua' (doo-WAH). For the dua', Ibraheem holds his hands open in front of his body, and prays to Allah for help or guidance.

The fast for Ramadan begins each morning before sunrise.

While his brother and sister sleep, Ibraheem joins his parents for an early breakfast to prepare for the day's fast.

During the month of Ramadan, Ibraheem gets up long before daylight. He has a good breakfast because he won't be able to eat again until after sunset. This early morning meal is called Sahoor (sah-HOOR).

Although Muslims are not required to fast until they are adults, parents encourage their children to try fasting. Fasting is hard. It is difficult to remember not to eat or drink anything during the day, especially when it is hot outside or when children have been playing hard. Ibraheem, however, has been keeping the Ramadan fast since he was six years old.

After Sahoor, Ibraheem makes wudu and then joins his parents for Fajr (FADJR), the first prayer of the new day. After the prayers are finished, Ibraheem goes up to his room to sleep a bit before he must leave for school.

When Muslim families pray at home, they do it the same way they do in the masjid. The men and boys stand in the front, with the women and girls behind them. Even at home, everyone faces in the direction of Makkah for the prayer.

Ibraheem and his brother, Ismael, attend an Islamic school located in the small buildings behind the masjid. Students from kindergarten through high school fill the classrooms. Ibraheem's mother and his aunts are teachers at the school.

The students at Ibraheem's school learn math, reading, English, social studies, and science. They also learn to read and write in Arabic and study Islam.

Muslim communities are building schools because they want their children to learn to read and understand the Qur'an and to learn about Islam and Muslim history. Muslim schools also make it easier for children to keep up the daily prayers, perform the fast, and follow other traditions in the Muslim way of life.

During recess, the students play basketball or soccer in the parking lot behind the masjid.

Although most of the classwork is done in English, Ibraheem and his classmates learn how to read and write in Arabic. When Muslim girls are about ten years old, they begin to wear head scarves and body-concealing clothing like their mothers.

During Ramadan, some girls in Ibraheem's class like to decorate their hands with painted henna designs. This widespread Muslim tradition was made popular in the United States by immigrants from many Muslim countries where these marks celebrate festive occasions.

17

Each day's fast ends as the sun goes down.

Before Iftar each night when Ibraheem breaks his fast, he eats a few dates. He likes to do this because he has learned that the Prophet Muhammad broke his fast with dates in days of old.

After going without food or drink since dawn, everyone looks forward to the meal at the end of the day. At sundown, they break the fast by drinking a little water and eating a few dates. After the Maghrib (MAH-grib) prayer, Ibraheem and his family enjoy the Iftar (if-TAHR) meal. Ibraheem's family likes to share this meal with other relatives and friends. When just the family is present, Ibraheem's mother likes to serve the meal in the family room. The whole family sits together on a blanket on the floor to eat. It is like having a picnic indoors.

For Ibraheem and his family, the changes in their daily schedule during Ramadan set this time apart from the rest of the year. Like other Muslims, they feel that this is a time when they are closest to each other, and closest to Allah.

Toward the end of Ramadan, Muslims spend more and more time in the masjid praying. During the last ten days of Ramadan, many Muslims spend entire nights in the masjid. It is during this time that the Night of Power occurs. Muslims believe that these prayers bring many blessings.

One of Ibraheem's favorite events during Ramadan is called Itekaf (ih-teh-KAHF) when he and his classmates spend the entire day and night in the masjid, totally focused on the worship of Allah. The students come to the masjid around the time of breaking the fast in the evening. They pray the Maghrib prayer and then eat Iftar together. Afterward, they do arts and crafts projects until time for the Isha prayer.

After the Isha prayer, they say a special prayer called Taraweeh (tah-rah-WEEH) with the Imam and all the other Muslims in the masjid. This special prayer is longer than any of the five daily prayers, often lasting for two hours or more.

After the prayer is finished, most people go home. The students, however, stay to worship, read the Qur'an, and work on arts and crafts projects. Those who get tired rest in sleeping bags in the masjid. Some children, however, don't sleep at all. They stay up all night until it is time for Sahoor. Ibraheem and his friends eat eggs, toast, bagels, and cereal before the dawn breaks. When the time to begin the fast comes, they pray the Fajr prayer together. Ibraheem says that Itekaf is like a big sleep-over at the masjid, and it's an event that he looks forward to all year.

The Night of Power

In the name of God, Most Gracious,
Most Merciful,
We have indeed revealed this (Message)
in the Night of Power.
And what will explain to thee
what the Night of Power is?
The Night of Power is better
than a thousand Months.
Therein come down the angels
and the Spirit* by God's permission,
on every errand: Peace!
This until the rise of the Morn!
–Qur'an 97

* The Spirit is usually understood
to be the Angel Jibreel.

Ibraheem's grandmother shows him how to mix the cookie dough by hand, just as she did when she was a child in Egypt.

Ibraheem's grandmother puts a mixture of dates inside cookies called kahk (KAHK) and oras (OH-ras).

Many families have special foods that they make at this time of year, especially sweets. Near the end of Ramadan, Ibraheem, his brother, Ismael, and his sister, Mariam, like to go to their grandmother's house to help bake special cookies for the Eid celebration. Eid is the holiday that marks the end of Ramadan. Everyone says these cookies taste even sweeter because by the time they are eaten, everyone has gone for so many hours without food.

Ghorayyibah

Ingredients:

1 cup butter (at room temperature)
1/2 cup sugar
dash of vanilla powder
   or 1 teaspoon of vanilla extract
2 cups flour
whole almonds
powdered sugar (optional)

Preheat the oven to 300 degrees. Cream the butter and sugar until the mixture is smooth. Add the vanilla. Mix in the flour. Beat the dough for at least five minutes to make it smooth. (Using your hands is best!)

Roll the dough on a floured board. The cookie dough should be about 1/4 inch thick. Use cookie cutters to make shapes. These cookies are traditionally cut into circles or rectangles. Press an almond in the center of each cookie if you like.

Place the cookies on a cookie sheet and bake for 10–15 minutes, until the bottom of the cookies are slightly browned. The cookies should be very light, so you will need to watch them carefully. Cool the cookies. Dust them with powdered sugar when you are ready to serve them.

Ismael and Ibraheem dip cookie dough in sesame seeds before they are baked.

Ibraheem and his brother arrange a variety of cookies on each plate. Ibraheem's family will serve these cookies to guests who come to visit during the celebration of the Eid at the end of Ramadan.

Mariam and Ibraheem help their mother wrap gifts for all the cousins who will come to celebrate the end of Ramadan at their house.

Muslims who live in different parts of the world have many different ways of celebrating Ramadan. In the United States, there is a great diversity among the Muslim population because people have moved here from all over the world. There can be different traditions even within a single family, as in Ibraheem's case. His mother's traditions come from Egypt, and his father's, from Bosnia.

Before the end of Ramadan, all Muslims have a very important responsibility to fulfill. Each family donates to the poor the amount of money it would take to feed the number of people in their family. For example, Ibraheem's family must give enough to feed five people, since there are five people in his family. Such gifts remind Muslims of the need to be generous with the wealth Allah has provided for them. This gift is called Zakat-ul-Fitr (zah-KAHT-ul-FITR). Muslims believe that their fasting is not accepted by Allah until the Zakat-ul-Fitr is given. Zakat is not a government tax, nor is it charity. Rather for Muslims it is a form of worship because it was commanded by God. Muslims believe that all wealth is God's bounty, and all that humans have comes from Allah.

Ibraheem's grandfather takes the children to shop for new clothes as they prepare for the end of Ramadan.

Celebrating the End of Ramadan

The end of Ramadan is celebrated with the Eid al-Fitr, which means the Feast of the Fast-Breaking. It occurs on the morning after the end of Ramadan, on the first day of the month of Shawwaal. When Ramadan ends, people are filled with happiness. They have met the challenge of fasting and are ready to receive the blessings that will come from it.

To determine the time of the Eid, people watch for the first new moon to shine in the heavens. Then they know that the time of fasting has come to an end. A date can be estimated in advance, but only the sighting of the new moon can mark the proper time for the celebration.

Beginning early in the morning, Ibraheem and his family, along with thousands of other Muslims, gather together for a special Eid prayer. This event involves every Muslim in the community. For this reason, the masjid is too small to accommodate all those who wish to participate. Many Muslim communities hold the prayers out of doors in parks if the weather permits, or inside a large covered stadium. On this day, Muslims want to be together to celebrate their faith.

This special morning begins with communal prayers called Salat al-Eid (sah-LAHT al-EED). These prayers give glory and honor to Allah and last much longer than the daily prayers. After praying, people gather at the homes of friends or relatives to celebrate.

In the Princeton area, there are so many Muslim families who wish to participate in the Eid al-Fitr prayer that the masjid isn't large enough. The people meet in the ballroom of a large hotel for the special prayers to end Ramadan.

After the Eid prayers are finished, it is time to celebrate the end of the fast. Everyone is happy to have completed the fast and fulfilled their obligations for Zakat. For the Eid al-Fitr, Ibraheem's family hosts a big family dinner. Relatives come from many miles away to be together on this special day. More than fifty people come, including grandparents, aunts, uncles, and many cousins. Many of Ibraheem's relatives have moved to the United States from Muslim countries such as Egypt, Bosnia, Turkey, and Syria.

The imam leads the people in the Eid prayer, followed by a sermon.

(Above) Ibraheem's grandfather enjoys some time with his granddaughter Halima.

(Left) The women in the family gather in the family room to pray.

(Below) Ibraheem and Ismael find time to play computer games with their cousins. Ismael holds a few dollars that he got from a family friend. Some Muslims give children gifts of money on this special day.

(Above) Ibraheem and Ismael join their father to greet guests who have come to their home to share their Eid celebration.

Dressed in their best clothes, the children enjoy the Eid al-Fitr because it is a time of feasting and fun. Even the youngest, however, pause to offer their prayers to Allah.

Every year on the Eid, Ibraheem's grandfather reads several passages of the Qur'an to his grandchildren. He hopes that they will grow up to love the message in this sacred book as much as he does.

(Above) There are lots of gifts for the children. Before they can be opened, however, the children play a quiz game. Ibraheem's mother and aunt ask questions about Islam and Ramadan. The team with the right answer chooses the next gift to open.

Ibraheem's sister, Mariam, opens a gift from her grandmother.

Although he is only nine years old, Ibraheem has succeeded in fasting like a grown-up. Once again, he has kept the Ramadan fast for an entire month. He and his father have read from the Qur'an each day. One day soon, Ibraheem hopes to be like his grandfather, reading the entire Qur'an from cover to cover during Ramadan.

By their faith in Islam, Ibraheem and his family have challenged themselves to live according to God's command. However, since they live in the United States, they are in a minority. Sometimes their ways are misunderstood by others. Still, they feel God has given them many blessings. On this special Muslim holiday, Ibraheem and his family are proud to follow a way of life filled with peace and submission to Allah.

Glossary

Allah: (ah-LAH) The name of God in Arabic.

asr: (AHS-er) The Arabic word for the prayer given from late afternoon until just before sunset.

dua': (doo-WAH) The Arabic term for a type of prayer, or supplication, in which a person asks Allah for help or a blessing.

Eid al-Adha: (EED al-UD-hah) The Feast of the Sacrifice, commemorating Abraham's faith on the tenth day of Zul-hijja.

Eid al-Fitr: (EED al-FITR) The Feast of the Fast-Breaking that occurs on the first day of Shawwaal as Ramadan ends.

fajr: (FADJR) The Arabic term for the prayer offered from dawn until just before sunrise.

Five Pillars of Islam: Five principles upon which Islam is based: Shahada (Declaration of Belief), Salat (Prayer), Sawm (Fasting), Zakat (Poor's Due), and Hajj (Pilgrimage).

hajj: (HAHJ) The Arabic term for a pilgrimage to the Kaaba in Makkah.

henna: A reddish brown natural substance used to color the skin in intricate designs.

Ibraheem: (ib-rah-HEEM) Arabic for Abraham, one of the first Prophets of God, also the father of Ismael, from whom the Prophet Muhammad is descended.

Iftar: (if-TAHR) An Arabic term for the meal at the end of each day during Ramadan that breaks the fast.

isha: (ee-SHAH) The Arabic word for the prayer offered at night.

Islam: (is-LAHM) A religion and way of life, whose followers believe in one God, Allah, and follow the Five Pillars of Islam.

Ismael: (is-mah-EEL) The first son of Ibraheem (Abraham) and an ancestor of Muhammad.

Imam: (ee-MAM) A leader of the prayer as well as the spiritual leader of a group of Muslims.

Jibreel: (Jib-REEL) An angel (Gabriel in English) who brought the revelations from Allah to Muhammad.

Kaaba: (KAH-bah) An ancient shrine in Makkah for the worship of Allah established by Ibraheem and Ismael in antiquity.

maghrib: (MAH-grib) The Arabic word for the prayer offered after sunset until daylight ends.

masjid: (MAHS-jid) The building where Muslims gather to pray together. It is also a meeting place for the Muslim community and often the site of a Muslim school.

minaret: (MIN-ah-rhet) A towerlike structure connected to a masjid, originally built as a place where a Muslim could call others to prayer.

mosque: The English word for a masjid.

Muhammad: (mu-HAHM-mad) The last Prophet of God, who lived in the seventh century and to whom Allah revealed the Qur'an.

Muslim: (MUS-lim) A person who believes in Islam and follows the Five Pillars of Islam.

Night of Power: One of the last ten nights of Ramadan, in which the Qur'an was first revealed to Muhammad. Muslims like to spend this night in the masjid, praying until dawn, believing that it brings many blessings.

prophet: A person sent by Allah to teach people God's laws.

Qur'an: (kur-AHN) The sacred book of Islam, in which the revelations of Allah to Muhammad have been written down for all generations.

ra'kah: (RAH-kah) One cycle of specific actions and words that comprise a Muslim prayer.

Ramadan: (rah-mah-DAHN) The ninth month in the Islamic calendar and the time of fasting. It is in this month that the revelations of the Qur'an to Muhammad began.

Rasul: (rah-SOOL) The Arabic term for Messenger.

revelation: Something that is revealed or shown to a prophet by God.

Sahoor: (sah-HOOR) The pre-dawn meal that provides a Muslim with sustenance before a day of fasting.

salah: (sah-LAH) The Arabic word for prayer.

sawm: (SAHWM) The Arabic word for fasting.

shahada: (shah-HAH-dah) One of the Five Pillars of Islam, a Muslim's declaration of faith that there is but one God, Allah, and that Muhammad is His Prophet.

surah: (SUHR-ah) The Arabic word for a chapter in the Qur'an.

wudu: (woo-DOO) The Arabic word for the ritual washing of the hands, face, and feet in preparation for the Muslim prayer.

zakat: (zah-KAHT) An Arabic term for the Poor's Due, which is one of the Five Pillars of Islam, a special form of which is Zakat ul-Fitr, which all Muslims must pay before the end of Ramadan each year.

zuhr: (ZUHR) The Arabic term for the prayer that is offered after midday until mid-afternoon.

Index